AT THE MERCY

Also by Libby Houston

A Stained-Glass Raree Show
Plain Clothes

At the Mercy

poems by

LIBBY HOUSTON

ALLISON & BUSBY
LONDON and NEW YORK

First published 1981 by
Allison and Busby Limited
6a Noel Street, London W1V 3RB, England
and distributed in the USA by
Schocken Books Inc
200 Madison Avenue, New York, NY 10016

British Library Cataloguing in Publication Data
Houston, Libby
At the mercy.
  I. Title
  821'.9'14   PR6058.084A/   80-40639
  ISBN 0-85031-347-3
  ISBN 0-85031-262-0 Pbk

Set in Monotype Perpetua
by Gloucester Typesetting Co. Ltd
Printed and bound in Great Britain
at The Pitman Press, Bath

Acknowledgements

Some of these poems were first published in the following magazines:

Bananas ("Faithful Dog", "A Cave", "Harborough Rocks", "Introduction to an Old Story", "On Location"); Doors ("The Kitchen Girl's Task"); Matrix ("Playing Time"); New Departures ("A Knot", "A House"); New Worlds ("Weather Clock"); Pick ("Nik at a Crux"); Slow Dancer ("Crying Wolf", "A Question of Ice", "Hedging and Ditching"); Smoke ("Centrifugalized in Finsbury Park"); Transatlantic Review ("The Adamant Soldier").

"Weather Clock" appeared in the Arts Council anthology New Poetry 1, and "Harborough Rocks" in the P.E.N. anthology New Poems 1977–78.

"Judging Lear" was commissioned by the Globe Playhouse Trust and published in Poems for Shakespeare: Vols 1–6, A Selection (1978).

"A Dragonfly" was commissioned for the BBC schools programme Stories and Rhymes and published in the accompanying pamphlet (1974, 77 and 78).

Thanks to many friends for encouragement and support, and in particular to Paddy Bechely, Alan Brownjohn, Carol Burns and Emma Tennant for commissioning poems I would not otherwise have written. Special thanks also, with apologies, to Anne Bristow, Michelle Gillam, Ruth Morozzo and Bob Pascall whose drawings could not in the end be used.

To Annette Road, London

My sullen landlady, my rough-tongued medium,
    have this for your dented treasure-tin
along with all the births, deaths, savagery and pleasure
    that had to fit to your measure,
and your green private jewelling I may guess again by the season—
    no less forget, no less remember, us, moved on.

Contents

The Cap of Invisibility

— See this? I'll let you into a secret:
   it's a *cap of invisibility*.

— A *what*?

— You heard.
   Remember Saturday night you left early?
   Well, I was last to go—too late for me, daft—
   and no moon, right? And just by the gate
   to the long field, a little noise; too high up, too
   slow for a small creature, no cows there this year yet,
   I thought. Shone my torch,
   on a *grey dress*, two white hands,
   holding, this—

— Come on come on show us let's see put it on—

— You don't believe me?
   All right then, watch, just keep watching—
   see? Right hand at the back, left at the
   front, I pull it
   down—

— It's bloody gone!
   Amazing!

   Can you still feel it?

— I can.

— Hey give us a go let's have a go do it again do it again!

The Kitchen Girl's Task

A demon took over Frank, chief
   at the café on the motorway:
arms akimbo, as midnight clicks, he
   summons one of the girls, says:

I want you to count the tealeaves
   we've used here today,
and I'll wait for the right answer.

The prince could not wait, he left her.
   Tears and the fumes of the bins
had sympathy from the clouds of morning.

The prince set out to find his enemies
   who would not wait for man or beast.
Regularly he wrote her letters,
   repeating her unchanging name.

One night, in a dream, she saw
   the little sodden leaves rise,
rank themselves in rows of ten.

She read his considerate lines:
   "How bright I remember your eyes
in all that dry glare."

"Today we picked up the scent again."
   "I've found true friends here!"
"We're having *Freedom*
   tattooed on our right wrists."

Sometimes she put down cloth or knife
   to wander within the boundary.
She would not have heard Rumpelstiltskin
   if he had shouted in her ear.

Silence for her became a rule;
   she was ashamed—and Frank was there
ordering her to wipe the stoves
   and wash the floor as usual.

After a while it came to her
   that no two leaves were identical.

The Adamant Soldier

He was an adamant
soldier
who left no kiss or
kind word
with a wife found wanting;
she is sobbing,
leaning on the latch,
door open,
barbed frayed—some golden—
streamers of himself
still trailed out passing her
and down.

Day night night day
then a halt;
for the face of her pleading
slips full-face across his
and he, dying,
cried out *I will come
back*, a hoarse
and ill-timed cry,
and night.

The dumb invisible
ghost can flow
through the locked door
for ever, a stale trick;
but the doors and walls
of her, as ice
melting and freezing,
slowly change places.
Dead he cannot judge
the key.

He found his old
coat on a hook
and made it fall;
the buttons clattering
down, she looks up,
goes to open
the wardrobe:
*I could make the boy
a winter jacket out of this,
and use the rest
for a rag-rug*—she laughs at herself—
if I ever get round to it.

Under the Greenwood

Under the greenwood a black dog lurches
nose to earth, the new growth's glow
catching him each time dark frees;

sidetracked by a briar he scratches,
clawing out the precious bird
leaf-buried by a child
who knew nothing of it alive,

and rolls and twists and whines,
and the coarse hairs of his spine
wipe out a scheme of time's
to shape for a child white treasure,
the same child, or another.

A Knot

Three men called at her farm for her
after their mid-day meal:

it was for the sake of another man's passion
that their blood was dry on the shingle
before that day darkened.

In the morning he laughed by the stable-door:
with evening his horse came riderless.

The ancient knife at her heart
she called down a longer night
on herself, and on the promised child:

and still his mother prayed
when her prayers no longer could be answered.

Travelling Downstream

Hemmed by a reed,
by a dressed stone checked,
dense bodies, their lithe braids
willow-swept, cloud-decked,
that drive light in their falling
through bedded rock as clay,
harnessed, harried,
grind and gnaw,
but fair and foul,
wi' speed and slaw
draw down
spring to firth, beck to mouth,
one way:

silver strands greet nut-brown hair,
midges raise frenzied monuments of air—
O take to the river, cast off! But forced or free
there's no change midstream downstream to the sea.

Some stick at the source a hand can dam
(tall as a bulrush the daisies by the brim),
one gives his orders—the engine-room
has him borne through the channel over a shot of rum—
who finds a full course,
or, finding it, can sense its measure?

Ant on a spinning leaf,
collier in the estuary,
swimmer, log, dead dog,
foam below the factory—

the neighbours who set out,
all unawares, together,
won't be meeting again.

This woman, and the seven mothers she is,
    drifts like turning sand:
  cloudburst, thaw, do what they will,
    she will lapse gently, to lie still
  where the outriders of the salt swell
    can never touch her hand;

    this married man, united
    father and son,
    rows himself on, on,
    in his prime translated
    to pistons his sweat greases,
    till the coast shrinks from his face—
    but all he registers
    is a lost variety in the near blur,
    and the glare has gone,
    and he himself is louder—
    was this what he intended?
    Remember? Might it have been
    easier?

A sunny crisis dips white flowers of
water-crowfoot under twigs like hair:
rowlock jammed, picnic squashed, one
oar lost—and just as the hour's up!
I can't quite reach it yet—Take care!

And the wide boom of rubbish riding
    west with the bright morning
    bears the blind white bottle
    to immortality:
  though worms destroy his body, yet
  in carnation-finished evening dress
he went to earth, eyes frozen at the dark
    his open legacy.

Down to the shallows, skirts tucked up,
children run, the buttercup
pollen gold on their white, to paddle:
when the river fills,
when the sea's hands unravel
the knitting from the hills,
a rapt child paddles still, who cannot get
so much as her knees wet.

I, I really shouldn't have come, I'm
sorry, I'm sorry, I promised I'd be
back before dinner—is there somewhere,
anywhere, is there, you could drop me?

But vessels and hands become interchangeable,
below the horizon boat and king burn together,
and the fisherman on the level bank does not yet know
the cruiser bearing his name foundered long ago.

O name by name bear down the rivers
name and song honouring would own—
known nameless thoroughfares
of kingfisher and swan,
that cling to straws
and shatter the face of the moon.

Cold rock to play them in, they dance the compass,
catching the random harvest in their coils:
one sea it was turned loose the rainers, raiders,
and waits at every gate to count the spoils.

Weather Clock

a clean and smooth hill
is gathered into a windmill.
under the glass the sails
throw out beams of light.

away round they go, backing
with the shift of the wind.
blue clouds keep their level
in dark, still lines.

down on the green by the well
a man with white shirt plain as paper
bends and straightens while side by side
his pale fists turn the winch.

one way he winds, and then the other,
making the rope quiver.
the bucket reaches neither parapet
nor, by his ease, water.

I am watching and weighing.
I have compassed his trick.
I have not shown myself
and need not speak.

the glass is beginning to fall.
I shall smoothe
my hair, my pinafore,
to the door.

A House

Two standing women are watchtowers
across the pillows of a bed;
wrestlers their eyes locked in a hold,

yellowed ceiling of a cold room.
Sleeper wake, within a breath, one whole
mouth. Sleep, let him, the other said,

do not do not cut peace from him
and both of us can place our love on him.
Wake and chance the pain, we can chance

your hate your leaving. One mother, one
lover, yellow light, an unwatched head,
will he wake of himself? Perhaps he is dead:

curtains pulled to, leaves tapping.
Into a dull girder equal force welds
their gaze, which can suspend him.

Crying Wolf

Beyond the pale, without the wall,
on the hillside, in the desert, crying *Wolf! Wolf!*
was that fable-boy hungering for a proof
of relevance—found after all sour, but worth
repeating, if only for the feel of spitting?

Was it his shouting the word
drew the wolf in from his horizon,
the blurred line of the wood—as if an
idea, once detached, will steer its
own course, hungry to be fact?

Last night, tonight, a child at home has learned
Ration your cries, your mother can tire—
soft as so much green grass that laps a weathered
stone inscribed *Depend on None.*

But suppose it the wolf's desire,
conceived but not yet born, that pressed the cry
from a boy who couldn't say why
and laughed like mad as he hid,
picked out clear like a deer in a gunsight?

*A liar will not be believed
even when he speaks the truth,*
a circle has it, where faces facing
nothing but faces can tangle moral
with excuse; this version,
only, *Cry wolf, the wolf is certain.*

Introduction to an Old Story

Where was it he picked her out?
  Some far-off kingdom across the sea.
"All my servants," he said,
  "shall be yours to command",
and the knots were firm and even there,
  not one would leave that net for her.

One island brought to another—
  O with a shadow to be proud of
  behind her on the water—
but she longs for her reflection
  to know what substance to hazard,
and the little waves scatter it,
catch and distribute her all the day long.

Thinks too much of herself. Too soon,
  it wasn't right. He'll find out.
A shame about his first, oh
  she was kind, rest her soul.
It breaks my heart to see
  a motherless baby smile.

She makes her condition:
  "But, I have to see myself
  before I can move
  even a finger surely."
She strokes a stray hair
into the perfect curve above her temple,

turns, turns to the king, her husband,
  her means, her only medium,
who giving her back herself might lay
her ready hand, her reaching hand
on the live current of his land,
  his strangers, with his own hand.

This was his error:
   he chose to be mirror
and thought it would answer;
that magic required of him
   its logical conclusion,
to frame her an open window,
   the arch of high heaven.

Did he listen? Did he hear?
   He settles across her eyes like low cloud
blocking the sun, he gazes
   ravenously and always satisfied
as the earth at its half of the tethered moon;
   silvered without a flaw.

And she can see neither him nor past him,
   only her reflection.
Wasn't this what you wanted?
   "It is a worse prison."
She dreads daring it with her moving hands:
   it shows no alteration.

What's become of the king?
   A fire-fixed slab on the wall.
The servants treasure a little girl,
   the counsellors govern well.
The barren queen plays her game
   bitterly, daring it with time

which holds the winning hand,
   his daughter's hand.
The pretty path comes out of the wood,
and nothing now between image and shadow
   but a dry fear, a fear of nothing
which will fight for nothing, tooth and nail.

The old tale moves into gear,
   sure of a happy ending.

A Question of Ice

Set down on a pale road patched with the sky,
January, before sunrise, behind us on a rise a row
of cold-windowed cottages backing away:

your eyes and mine—deny if you like—
the burst of little birds, their tattered cries,
carried from field to sky to us each other—

as if it should matter, now!

With all the snow by then down,
lying or pressing down,
blue lines of the furrows
begin to swallow, have begun.

Your blue eyes, your cold glass,
my window, your being, flooding
all these outlines to the rim, those
grey homes, blue fields, those black trees,
this road south, this breaking day,
as far as the horizon, that running
horizon, yourself my horizon, I
dumb beside you, bloodless morning.

Nothing in this world
to stop that snow vanishing,
your road home; and one of mine
stopped in its tracks there, frozen.

Sixteen years glance from a train—

blue ground, white hill, black trees,
that curve of grey-faced cottages on a rise,
level line of that road,

lines, lines, these lines—but,
that ice should preserve its own self too,
as fresh, as hard, as unrequired?

Faithful Dog

And there the little dog shall starve
sitting a wet November through
by the raw lumps of clay that smother
his master's bed,
no longer last in the new ground, sheaved
chrysanthemums, and poppies, dead
by a course fixed as the stars which rules
him too, unfed.

Little grey snotty-eyed dog, with your trembling
rib-cage, ingrown tail—
the mortal hand that was used to beat you
for rich snatched street-corner tastes
and fork your tin,
that fondled you for sitting and lying down
without demanding that you die for the Queen
or learn to count, walk on two legs,
or herd, or hunt,
and sometimes received your ecstasy like a brick
to build the walls of purgatory, a maze
where you might round the corner on such crimes
as ruining nylon, scratching paint,
has transformed you, now and for all time.

> *Bring your stick to the gate*
> > *and leave it there*
> *like a visiting warrior*
> > *his spear;*
> *I will give you a collar*
> > *made all of leather*
> *and pull you where you would not go.*

Not a long story, but beyond it
a woodcut shows
a tray of stones
pierced by a bony arm—
that troubled hand
stretching up and reaching out against all nature
to pat a faithful head
(no wife or children carried a head so faithful,
winding up the estate, and growing);

or in one copy
the absorbed hand of a colouring child has
called up the image
of a starving dog brought back to life
by a bony hand with flesh still on it,
that swings between
rape and offering;

or, on a white screen like endpapers,
a film-clip swims into possession with: evening,
a neat man turning in at the funnel of the gates;
close-up by the grave: he rummages in a bag,
puts down butcher's scraps, backs, smiles seeing them
wolfed, and wipes his hands. Cut to: interior,
sitting beside his wife now on sofa—it's a
television break, looking round at her, he starts
"I forgot to tell you, on my way home tonight I . . ."
with a little shrug, and the same smile rising.

Is there room in the story for a boy
running into the kitchen to say *Mum
can I keep him can I keep him found him
lost in the cemetery*—
"Poor thing, doesn't he look hungry,
what do you think, dear?"
or, "What the hell were you doing there?"

or, was there room out among the marble
headboards for a dog
who chose like a god
to shield a would-be god till the last
judgement from the judgement
of his peers and no less
against tears too prompt
with the right answer
that rule the vision blurred?

The little dog expands and shrinks,
shrinks and expands, and no one sees
what isn't there;

somewhere on the Elysian Fields
bewildered man and bewildered dog
come face to face, and, by no more than
that, forgive each other

and between the shit in the grass
and the pinpoint larks, the wild
blown doves, now they run, roll, run riot,
and now are, and never.

A Cave

having left the light
leaving no sign a man untraceable
under the earth confronts
a torrent still as ice an end the vaulted ceiling
pours down past his feet, the black welling
the cold draught the water cold as marble
described impassable

so he turns back or he dives under

all he brought with him a reckoning
of a far side could be a mirror image
and not so far as to burst him:
even chance and a quick proof face him

"risking his life with candle and matches"
no, all his mothers' cares have missed
the black crack in the sun by the rowan tree,
and no danger here from bravery

if he dives under

that some have stumbled on crystal fields
confirmed hypotheses of sunless seas
and one touched the flanks of a clay bear
untouched twenty thousand years

that his name might earn a name—and the looks
the well-equipped follow-up team exchange
seeing the place as he must have weighed it—
so much sugar dissolved: the surface faces
him and what brought him, come to dive he will

the splash is swallowed whole

in cold in black eyes shut he feels
no foothold nothing the cruel keel:
a wedge of air his fingers find
before his mouth can, that was it

black air black rock black water meet part
play with him, him his floating hair
and blood as black, the game a bitter fight
with nothing to call enemy: *Jesus Christ!*
Shit! he lands a monster in the dark he grins
making fire there, but that was more than it

and what was lit that ne'er was lit?

passage chamber and stream
cold sharp wet grey an end a massive boulder-fall
whose tremor never stirred the grass:
his theory triumphed, that was all

> *With the Queen of Elfland Thomas rode*
> *starless night and rivers of blood:*
> *in this land ye sall haud your tongue,*
> *speak ye word ye'll not return.*
> *Seven years of blood and night he rode*
> *and all that time spoke never a word.*
>
> *She reined in by the Eildon tree,*
> *a gift she gave as she bade farewell:*
> *Thomas, a tongue that can never lie—*
> *no use to him to sing or sell*
> *or what he already had she gave—*
> *for as I say so must it be.*

but to dive back does not unact the act;
to make it true to himself he need not tell
as nameless still he even forgetting it
cannot be now who he was:
it was the mirror image fixes
the colours come into him from a lightless prism

he is drawn he is less he steps from the cave

the gold light the red of the berries held at him
are no more for him than the bruises to his bones:
the grey the mauve clouds tending their shadows
cross the contained body of the fell

At the Mercy

In Memory of Mal Dean, 1941–74

Years build their wall at the back of me
shrinking their days down to coloured dice
to fit the fixed height of it, my own:

it's been two years of days, three years and four
since the day you died, the day I heard
your breath stop like a clock—and the black
pit of your mouth that sighed of itself, your wild
eyes that wouldn't close, the pillow I took with me home.

And six in the morning began this part, mine,
the news of it—how to meet
the contortions of condolence, pity and awe
in the light of what I saw:

for, sure in the face of fact you would
come through all right, it was dying I saw you
win, come through all right, pass on, depart
this life, not end—though I couldn't say you slept
who, shrunk to a matter of breathing, flat,
the ignominy of it, could say, and your undrugged
eyes alight, of the hard grey table where you lay,
My bed's like a horse carrying me away—

too far by then to think of looking back
to say good-bye—I couldn't call, stood back
lest you looked back, all the fear that rose
to permeate, to undo you, eagerness swept out—
celeriter cucurrit ille noctis equus! Only your eaten
body lapsed at last, nothing else like rest or peace.

And what am I doing—talking to, telling, you, who either
know or need no knowing, now so long in the ground? Was I
wanting to catch at you still, after all? No, rather,
for all I was safe on the sidelines, I'm saying, must lay it
before you, first, that it was no pitiful madness

when at six, Sunday, February, the morning you left me
caught out by death that I least expected
I thought, Is this what we're afraid of?
Why have we been afraid? Did I cry? If I did at all
it was at this word my head brought me: miracle,

and that moment, suddenly felt, for me,
the breath of that joy that blessed you
the night you stood over me
as I lay awkward, dealt with, among machinery,
at odds with the animal of my unkenned body,
watching your first child born—

we were apart then, yes, as this morning, I
wandered in men's ward, light from a white sky
on striped pyjamas, first rounds of tea, the trolley,
"Does he take sugar?", my head bewildered, filled
with the wild sweet gallop of your rushing to meet death,
to find no doubt of something ordinary
to call immortality, not a grain, not a speck—

and how to receive the anguish of those who had lost you,
unfinished parts of themselves for you still in their hands,
thinking, "God, may I die like that"? The ceremonies of Easter
close on your heels passed by, but I had glimpsed
redemption a human act the road you went ,
that jammed rejection, left nothing to resent.

That birth, it had fixed me in pain I couldn't believe,
foxed by some streak of reluctance across my own nature—
for less than a day: how I grudged you your vision
spent by that jaded expelling, and sweetness
surprised me no less, flowing in with the milk to my breast,
dividing us then, again—that fills me now with shame.

Can these terrible gifts come near to matching, how they
shout down the days' years we're to complete, alone,
each one? Must respect one another or kill, why kill?
Or why kill oneself trying to prove it wrong?
Coming graced then with the power of sharing
what at such cost not one would dare to ask for,
nor, mind's ease nearer, wish for?

This is beyond justice, beyond comparing—
the gift of release from the prison of human caring.

Sunlight on water, green leaves at the spring,
reflected light on honey-coloured stone:

between my ears and eyes as they registered,
my reason's processing, and the clichés, words,
these words, threadbare, dull, stale—stubborn enough,
this untranslated labour, where's the good in it?

But if I spelled some ancient name for yours,
set centuries and seas
to cut you from a room in Holloway,
how could it signify?
Poetry's my usage;
yours was the unimaginable fixing image.

So, is it mine? Is it mine
to tell at large, invite
the world in the booth to stare at you dumb, and me?
Oh poets can lie, they can modify
for a friend, trap, meal or a halo—so can I.
In your sleep once you said suddenly,
Never take money from a dead man's arse,
laughed!—I laugh now—No, I was a child
of absence, loss, waste; what good I made of death I heard
in its full cry back at the living, held,
the news of all heroism stood, and like a shield,
to face fire and ice, torture, guns, stones, men, fate,
or the rising Christ Himself for us always, and at the heart
faith, love maybe, but I see choice the key, that distancer
that coloured me in those acts so rich—
and nothing like this,
without choice, without an enemy, private sufficiency
among the stained plastic in a régime of care:

for in real life death I accepted to leave in its place
a lightless stone, an untouchable blank, despair
a priest it was promised me;
to find there joy—oh was no
grief-stopping thanks of mine for a finish to what pain,
it was yours, your own translation, unlike you, out of your hands
and no more meant for me than the light of that dawn, any dawn
—how should I hoard it for myself then,
and not be false and not be mean?

One day years ago
in the park on the hill after a fall of snow
expecting the sheer coat and gift of it we found
a full thaw that welled up out of the ground

at a touch, ran then with fountains at our feet,
rolled as it welled and ran, white vanishing
before us, the clear strands running down
and all the hillside's grass at rest the greener.

In real life we could hate too, wither and hurt,
eat, drink, and kiss; I can curse
too, the course of things, myself, our idiot
ignorance, cry, and dance, the children nurse
grievances, lark too, and sing;
and still there is this, like a rock, like a spring:

that, with the voice of death in you
telling you cower,
nod with a traded mind or rage out the hour,
you should be weighed, not found wanting,
and, equal, come into the power
to die alive, run on without a break, so tuned
that keeping pace so with mortality
I saw at once victory
and prize, then, now—and now;
now, braced for good-bye, almost I can see
this grace, its reach eternal, having no time nor need
even for that dear, treacherous formality—

(not unto us Lord, *non nobis Domine* . . .)

As the year curves
I catch the swifts with something of your eyes:
one day they're gone,
black into grey ground as time blows.
Now I have dressed this stone.
May nothing ill come near the way you're on;
may I see my own.

Judging Lear

Logic's hard lines have pressed
the flowers uncoloured, lace to dust,
danceable music stone:
three sisters, pared down
for the day's sacrifice, face
marble, a dear throne.

The awkward game begins,
logic in the chair, no blessing
asked and no grace said—
but grace can, creeping in by the old man,
plant there the bold gambit
he misinterpreted:

for though moved, inside and out, slow as
lead, alone, naked, right to the dark ground
where extremes as they meet
can cross, he is still a child (he also has)
playing counter to the rules the judged pair,
keeping the game open, did not cheat.

Fools, while he leans he knows, blocking that voice
silence has, let him, lest innocence lose
the match to logic and grace's
clinching alchemy, plead even to proving
insanity, rip up the board and smash
players and pieces,

parrying blame with a blame splendid as the
ancient swords that killed by name—as if
heaven's walls must mother turn gate
for the mere beating; or as if fixed in spite
to fall, by dragging down dearest one may
make it seem fate.

All alike stone, broken, the gold the sand:
the base emotions Plato banned
have left a radio-active and not radiant land.

Harborough Rocks

A man in breeches, gear a bright skirt, picked out,
bridges, rope held by a thread, the flowering rain:
where we left off, and when, and which of us, pick up again

and where, low crags blocked off at the foot as well by bad light,
white: that we each were there then as thin spun as the thread,
anchor, if I had got the job, or not met you now dead

begin to run, like ants, uncovering, I put the stone back
to resurrect what pattern in black I presume, do not presume,
not I on this date, bridging this little particular gloom:

brightness contained by grey, wet, a red apple lying in a drab
tangle, for picking up, for how long, where we left off, ropes coiled,
secured, to carry off: when I stood life on this rock it held.

Playing Time

Image in a black and white photograph,
for ever laughing and for ever young,
a girl in a black and white bathing suit
was me, pleased pleasing, and clock years gone.

Bare running feet in love with gravity
playing packed sand, like an air, for the air,
I, I know then, couldn't see
this moment holding its place
complete, untouchable, like this print is—
frame in a sequence long as life is;
or wishing, a poisoned shirt
as easily shed as a shirt;
or how, even as wide, to trust
such updraught as a low cliff gave us

and that original sin is just
a burdened alias for the ground bass
of human being—figured anywhere
earth is: the digesting riddled soil
dark constant out of which, after all,
all stems rise year after year unpropped,
climb flower and ripen and die back, not dropped,
and not I think laid low
by reckless hope, blind wan hope, jaw
set, out to better the clock by a pole-vault.

Outside the picture, above the hands
that held, and hold, the camera, the hill
now I imagine rasped by winter is still
yellow with primroses—higher a milk-white
fulmar, lightest of skiers, balanced on light,
at the same time falls from the air
swallowed into a stony lair—
and away across the sand
the black and white image of a clock can dart,
alien as a plover, respectable as a crab.

On Location

This was on Skye—the black-haired spaniel,
first, in the corrie, and then my mother with her
shepherd's old boots, you dropped, shed, forging ahead to climb
the Inaccessible Pinnacle of all things, with a roadmap,
telling her to wait, cold, lately-wed, at the foot there, where
the mountain-cloud received you out of her sight.

I led the Great Tor on the Gower last summer,
and at the top, in the sun, among flowers, looking down
on a black-backed bird flying high below me
and the clear deep-water covered sand, I suddenly saw
you, with your arms wide, reckless, glorious
on pinnacles above the sea or clouds
in the pre-war photographs, or one—one in particular
looking down on you at the top, so small, not up—
as if I'd been expecting unawares
you, whom I don't remember, to be there
to welcome me with a voice I'd like to recognize.

It was when your feet no longer touched
rock, or indeed the earth—when you were far far higher,
telling her, reckless in keeping, only to wait,
that presumed dead you vanished quite.
I suppose you too fell like Icarus, made to swallow
all your presumption in the seconds of spinning
down for deep water with a trail of black and fire—
the dazzling figure in that photograph
might equally have been gathered like Elijah
into a fiery chariot, to mount still higher,
doffing the body at last the quicker to rise.

Flat snaps, my father, and black and white at that,
giving me my leads, I follow, older
than you were, ever—measuring my reach
to make a guess at yours, at least.
Bruises and blood show up in close-up and colour.
Cold wind, a cold scent; waiting around gets colder.

Nik at a Crux

A red spot like a ladybird
on grey knuckles, a fixed gauntlet
the rock buttress: Nik's helmet,
and he then stretched on the stepless stair there
rain had begun to corrupt for me,
two hours away

and down, now, by the van selling tea
in the lay-by the rest of us, rain-dulled
lake on a level, the soft-edged canopy
closing in, erasing, scaling done, the slabs, the blocks
have scaled down all of us
to spots against grey,

"Do you take sugar?" and I think I hear him right,
"The best time, now, that summer, remember?
Before last? August, it rained a solid fortnight?
Three fishermen in the lake there up to their
waists, me in my van here and nothing else
but the sheep and the rain . . ."

I don't turn though, clamped, suddenly,
in a vigil to see you safe now, silly as touching
wood, knowing too though the burnished root-crook—
make out the matchstick tree of it—hand you home
the long descent still, darkening now,
false paths, loose shale—

and you could trip on a molehill! This strange caring
jams the door wide though, till I should recognize
till magnified out of all definition another, nearing,
roadside stance for me, my own children
out on my known far trickier ground,
out of earshot, late,

when I must turn away, holding my plastic cup
with greater faith than for you, Nik.

Hedging and Ditching

Here is a man who is
hedging and ditching.

I not understand—
how you say "hedging",
to cleave so sure how is this?

How you say "ditching"
to clean and fit make
for tomorrow, maybe she never come?

The Dragonfly

There was once a terrible monster
lived in a pond, deep under the water.

Brown as mud he was, in the mud he hid,
among murk of reed-roots, sodden twigs,
with his long hungry belly,
six legs for creeping,
eyes like headlights
awake or sleeping;
but he was not big.

A tiddler came to sneer and jeer
and flaunt his flashing tail—
Ugly old stick-in-the-mud
couldn't catch a snail!
I'm not scared—
when, like a shot,
two pincers nab him, and he's got!

For the monster's jaw hides a clawed stalk
like the arm of a robot, a dinner fork,
that's tucked away cunningly till the last minute—
shoots out—and back with a victim in it!

Days, weeks, months, two years and beyond,
fear of the monster beset the pond;
he lurked, grabbed, grappled, gobbled and grew,
ambushing always somewhere new—

Who saw him last? Does anyone know?
Don't go near the mud! But I must go!
Keep well away from the rushes! But how?
Has anyone seen my brother? Not for a week now—
he's been eaten
for certain!

And then, one day, it was June, they all saw him.
He was coming slowly up out of the mud,
they stopped swimming. No one dared
approach, attack. They kept back.

Up a tall reed they saw him climbing
higher and higher, until
he broke the surface, climbing still.

There he stopped, in the wind and the setting sun.
We're safe at last! they cried. *He's gone!*

What became of the monster, was he ill, was he sad?
Was nobody sorry? Had he crept off to die? Was he mad?

Not one of them saw how, suddenly,
as if an invisible knife had touched his back,
he has split, split completely—
his head split like a lid!
The cage is open. Slowly he comes through,
an emperor, with great eyes burning blue.

He rests there, veils of silver a cloak for him.
Night and the little stars travel the black pond,
and now, first light of the day,
his shining cloak wide wings, a flash, a whirr,
a jewelled helicopter,
he's away!

O fully he had served his time,
shunned and unlovely in the drab slime,
for freedom at the end—for the sky—
dazzling hunter, Dragonfly!

Centrifugalized in Finsbury Park

Hey I just had a go on one of them
things! Didn't notice it had a name,
but anyone could see what it was going to do to you—

something like a giant-size round biscuit-tin without a lid
made of wire-netting, and all around the inside,
niches, like for statues, 30 or so, like coffins, only
upright, and open of course with the kind of lattice—
with a padded red heart at head-height.

Paid 25p, got myself a niche, and stood and waited
with a little chain dangling across my hips,
until it was full, the gate shut, the music started
and the thing began to whirl.

It wasn't the stomach, it was what to do with the head:
no good looking down, but if you let your head back
it felt as if it was going to go on going back, or off—
a bit peculiar, shut my eyes to get through that.

And as it whirled, the whole thing turned on end,
more or less vertical—well, I'd seen that right from
the park gates and couldn't believe it, which was why—
and opening my eyes again then, just found myself
lying there—lying down face up, lying up face down
over the whole fairground!

And it didn't make you scream like the top of the Big
Wheel, but smile—look up and everyone else is standing there,
hanging there, smiling, look down and you might as well be a lazy
bird on the wind, though I did forget I could let go,

and the only strange feeling was,
every time you were on the down side hurtling up again,
you left the skin of your face behind for a second.
You know I've never dared try anything quite like that
before, and it was just very nice!

And when it slowed down and sank down, and all of us
were ordinary upright, and unhitched our little chains,
I only staggered a couple of times, disappearing
on ground level into the dark—and nobody was sick.

Scales

I came in from the garden—
that moon, it was not hidden—
and all I had was taken,
or all I had was given.